Whispers of the Soul

Anjannabet Toro

BookLeaf Publishing

Presentation by *BookLeaf Publishing*

Web: www.bookleafpub.com

E-mail: info@bookleafpub.com

ISBN : 9789394788886

First edition 2022

DEDICATION

This book is dedicated younger me. Stay strong, it doesn’t last forever.

ACKNOWLEDGEMENT

Thank you Jesús, Kiara and Tashira. You guys always pushed me to be myself even when I couldn't, and you are still here to see it. Thank you Carlos and Kei, for completing me.

PREFACE

When she couldn't anymore, she'd go to made-up worlds

They're here

As the clock ticks down,
My mind gets crowded.
As the wind grows cold,
My thoughts get heavy.
And as the last ray of sunshine flares up,
My demons arisen.

I think I'm home

You're like a peaceful walk on a forest,
the moment the sunset gives way to night,
a comforting lull of ocean waves.
You feel like a star-filled night,
or the silence between two mountains,
like a field full of Callas and sweetness in the air.
You're my breath of air as I was drowning,
an answer to a question never asked,
you're the feel and smell of Home.

The Woods

The wind caresses me,
The leaves celebrate,
That I'm here, finally.
The creatures say my name,
Poppy, Poppy, Poppy.
A chant, a welcoming,
A healing.
The arrival of the sad child,
Where I belong, home, my family.

A final fantasy

He plays my body like the chords of a cello
a sweet lament coming from his fingers.
The moan of my strings rise up
a song so sad, yet so beautiful.
A melody created of love found
between two souls lost in the abyss.

Books

This emptiness inside me
that only books can fill...
Temporarily.

In my Dreams

I wonder,
if you dream of me as I dream of you.

Not alone

Alone,
but surrounded.
Darkness,
clouding my senses.
Drowning me,
relentless.

A hero's speech

I am your hope,
key and solution.
I am your shield.
But most importantly,
I am your weapon (to be wielded)
and nothing more.

Am I, dying?

My soul is pruning,
slowly dying.
Round and round it goes
no longer fighting.

Fakes

I am surrounded by materialistic people,
ones who care how good a car looks.
Surrounded by good liars,
who will twist things for their benefit,
Who will pretend to be your friend for a number.
And when asked for help,
will pretend you never did.

Go away

I dreamt you took it away,
everything I wanted,
everything I loved.
Why were you so jealous?
Why did you rip it all apart?
Why couldn't you stay in the past?
Torturing me 'till the present.
Can't I move along?

I don't want to be insecure anymore.

Breathing

One breath, two breaths,
flowers bloom.
Three breaths, four breaths,
the Sun croons.
Five breaths, six breaths,
the leaves move.
Seven breaths, eight breaths,
the cold looms,
but time is motionless,
it tortures me.
Fool.

Depression

Silence,
my brain screams silence.
100 mph thoughts,
all silent.
It latches on my throat,
a silent killer,
murderous,
unforgiving,
relentless.

Depression: Part 2

I'm drowning in my own emotions.
My thoughts are unsettled and won't leave me alone.
The world is pushing down on me.
I scream and scream and scream,
but no one looks at me.
I just realized,
my thoughts aren't loud enough.

Disassociate

I can feel myself drifting,
losing the sense of reality.
The other me taking over,
a shell to protect my sanity.
From what? I can't tell.
The nice voice inside my head
has been quiet lately.

Love burns

His love is like a summer day;
warm, sunny and full of life,
but you'll get sunburned if you spend too much
time outside.

Wisp

I want to breath again.
No worries inside my mind,
no thoughts consuming me.

Music is...there

My soul bleeds
alongside the notes
played by a violin.
My tears fall
as the piano keys are being pressed.
The music drowns the physical pain,
even if just for a little bit.

Harmony

As his eyes met mine
and compliments fell from his lips;
As he reached for my cheek
and I slowly leaned into it,
I felt alive again.
For I'd heard the simplest words
and they planted seeds of life and hope inside.
And I knew...
I knew I'd do anything to be by his side.

It's all on you

I wake up to darkness
a ceiling of branches over my head,
the moonlight fighting to shine in between.
As I get up,
I feel the silence, stifling.
The trees are quiet
A presence lingering,
foul memories bestowing.
Before I can get ahead
a hand comes and holds me.
Turned around, I see my reflection
an uncanny precision of imperfections on my
skin

How can I show my love

I say the words from miles away
hoping that the wind grabs hold of them
and takes them your way.
But the wind, Oh treacherous wind!
Takes them the other way
to be taken by leaves
and use my love
for photosynthesis.

CPSIA information can be obtained
at www.ICGtesting.com
Printed in the USA
BVHW031400140922
646893BV00014B/1186

9 789394 788886